Table of Contents

INTRODUCTION

Blindly following your passion is a recipe for financial disaster. But if you learn just a little bit about how business and passion fit together in the modern age, you can realistically monetize the things you care about. That's a popular phrase, but it's terrible advice. If that were true, then the phrase "starving artist" wouldn't exist..It's terrible advice because it isn't grounded in reality. But it can be if you approach your passion intelligently and with a respect and understanding of how money and passions are related. To begin, we need to define both of these things.

10 WAYS TO TURN YOUR PASSION INTO PROFIT

1. Write About Your Interests

One of the simplest ways to go from doing something you love to profiting from it is to write about it. Most people have some sort of writing experience — students write essays, adults write resumes and cover letters, etc. Here are a few different ways to write about your interests, and in turn, make money.

Start a Blog

A simple way is to start a blog around the topic you are knowledgeable and excited about. However, profit is usually something that beginning bloggers have to wait for until they get their website traffic numbers up. Having said that, with proper SEO, excellent content, and some hustle, it's definitely possible to build a six-figure blog in just a year. With blogging, most money is made through affiliate marketing and ad networks. Once you have a following on your blog, you could also start using other ideas from this list, such as creating a product, to enhance your profit even more.

Write a Book

Another option is to create an ebook or write a physical book. You can self-publish and sell it through channels such as your own website, social media, and Amazon. It's easier than ever to self-publish, and if you aren't a designer and want a professional-looking cover, then you can search on websites like Upwork to easily hire someone for a one-off project. Or, if you'd like to give it a try yourself, have a look at simple design programs like Canva.

Freelance Writing

If you aren't interested in starting your own website or writing a book, you could always write for others. Pitch newspapers, magazines, or other blogs on the topic you're an expert in. Writing stories or informative pieces on a topic you're interested in really won't feel like work at all. It's easier than you think to find online writing jobs and beginner freelance writing work, and the pay can be quite good depending on the publisher.

2. Become an Expert Speaker

Another way of turning passion into profit is to become a public speaker. There are tons of different events that happen every year around the globe, on a wide variety of topics. Many of these events are looking for either established speakers in the industry or people who are incredibly passionate and knowledgeable about the topic, but haven't got their foot in the door — just yet. While some of the very first speaking events you do might be unpaid or at a lower rate because of your lack of experience, the more you go to these events, the more recognized and accomplished you'll become, which in turn leads to a higher income.

Over time, you may start to get invited to more significant events, which will not only pay more, but help grow your audience and brand presence. If you aren't a huge fan of speaking in front of large audiences, there's another option. These days, many speaking events are actually held online.

Starting out with a few online events can help give you a confidence boost and can be a good practice run for in-person public speaking seminars.

3. Create a Product

To turn your passion into profit, you could also create a product. And, of course, these days you can create both a physical product and an online one as well.

Digital Products

One route to consider is a digital product, which is the best idea considering so much of the world is online. These products could be in the form of PDFs, booklets, printables, video tutorials, cheatsheets, or something else that has to do with the industry you're excited about.

Physical Products

Another option is to look into physical products. This could be done with drop shipping if you want to make items like t-shirts, sweatshirts, bags, cups, or framed art. A physical product could also include something that you feel could be invented to help out the industry.

Creating Tech Products

Technology could be another way to make money if you're wondering how to monetize your passion. You could create an app, plug-in, video game, or some other sort of downloadable tech product that you could sell. Anything that fills a gap in the market and could help other people in the industry.

4. Create a Community

Community building is another excellent way to profit from your passion. Luckily, no matter your interests, this can be applicable. This includes if you're a graphic designer, yogi, fashionista, surfer, culinary chef or baker.

In the Go Forth series I mentioned earlier in this article, Tony Hawk says: "If you can find something you absolutely love doing and is your meaning for living and you can turn that into a business, that's it, that's the top of the dreams right there." Imagine doing the activity you love while being surrounded by like-minded people and making an income from it! There's no better way to turn passion to profit.

For example, if you absolutely love yoga, you could create a yoga retreat to build a community with others that have similar interests as you. Of course, not only would you be surrounded by fellow yogis, but you would charge people to attend and in turn, earn an income doing something you love. You'll come out of the experience with new friends, and will have a new community that you can connect with in the future if you host more retreats or have products to sell. Other community ideas include running guided tours (if you love travelling, sports, or history, etc.), hosting cooking classes, running surf camps, or setting up co-working or co-living spaces. Build a community, and surround yourself with people in your niche. This is a fun way to go from passion to profit!

5. Become a Coach or Consultant

If you're wondering how to monetize your passion and love being a leader and helping others, consider becoming a coach or consultant on the subject you are enthusiastic about. This can be a great way to make money. Consultants, because they specialize in a subject, actually can charge quite a bit for their services. As you gain more of a reputation and begin to garner testimonials, you'll also be able to raise your rates. As time goes on, you could even start a coaching group or mentorship program where you help other people in a larger community.

The great thing about being a coach or consultant is that you can easily offer these services from anywhere in the world, which opens up your potential client base. If you're located in New Jersey in the USA, you could offer to coach digitally to people in the United Kingdom and Canada while offering in-person services in your state or surrounding area. If you're interested in home decor, you could be an interior design consultant. People passionate about social media could be marketing consultants, and those who love food could be culinary consultants.

6. Start Making YouTube Videos

Thanks to the internet, turning passion into profit is a lot easier now than it was thirty years ago. There are thousands of people doing what they love, filming it, and uploading videos to platforms like YouTube. Just think about it. How many people on YouTube do you watch? There are many creators who share their passions through their videos, only to end up being a huge success from their videography a few years later!

On YouTube, any hobby and interest can be turned into profit, with income earned through ads and sponsors (among other ways). Travel fanatics can make travel vlogs or documentaries. Rock climbers can make videos about their climbs and vlog the whole experience. Chefs can start a cooking show and post a video online. Those who love the great outdoors can create useful videos about survival situations, fishing, camping, and more.

To turn your passion into profit, YouTube is a great avenue to consider. When it comes to video quality, you don't even need to buy a super-expensive camera. All you need is a phone or a camera on a computer. The same goes with editing, nothing special is needed for editing a video. Use the free video editing software that comes on your computer when first starting out. Your personality and enthusiasm shining through the video will make people subscribe!

7. Create a Course

It's easier now than ever to create a course. If you're tech-savvy or are able to follow along with online tutorials, you don't need to hire someone to help you. Courses today can be either online or in-person, but they're usually online just for the ease of it. Online courses are very simple to make. This can be particularly helpful to genres that can have "how-to" tutorials, like gardening, website design, cooking, or fashion.

There are many great course platforms online that are affordable. Some more popular ones include Teachable, Thinkific, and Podia, among others. Goats On The Road uses and recommends Teachable for online courses. With programs like this, you're able to create a course, and upload it to the platform. Then, people can sign up at any time and go through the materials at their own pace. Most courses include text-based media and video as well. Plus, extra learning material should also be included, such as monthly calls with your students, a workbook, access to a VIP Facebook group, or weekly homework as they go through the course to stay on track.

8. Become an Investor

To make money from your passion, you could also consider being an investor. This might be more applicable to people who have a bit of extra cash to put into their side hustle. But, it can easily pay off in the long run if you invest in the right type of businesses. Most investors will find businesses or startups that are in the industry they're most interested in. As an example, if you care for the environment, maybe you'd find a startup business that creates eco-friendly products. Or, if you have an eye for fashion, maybe there's a clothing company that needs a partner. If the company is a success, you could make a nice return on your investment — while being a part of helping a small business grow.

9. Network, Network, Network

Believe it or not, but networking can be a great way to profit from your interests. You never know who you might connect with that will help you on your journey. This is even more true if you aren't necessarily sure just how you will make money from your passions — yet. You can network through social media, with friends and family, on platforms like LinkedIn, or even through your past employers. Always keep business cards with you when attending events, too, because you never know when that card will come in handy. As the successful sales trainer and author Grant Cardone says, "It takes contacts to make contracts."

Maybe the person next to you at an event is looking to start a business in the exact niche you are, and would love to partner with you. Perhaps a friend of a friend is looking for an investment in something you are looking to get involved with. Or, maybe you meet someone who can offer a wealth of information and guidance with getting your new business off the ground! Meet people, be genuine, and collaborate where you can.

10. Host an Event

Last but not least, you could also consider hosting an event around whichever topic you are interested in. Events can be a great way to make money and raise awareness for your passion project or business. It can also be a perfect way to connect with other people with similar interests. This form of turning your passion into profit can be highly successful if you put effort into marketing. Of course, having some sort of a following and contacts before you plan the event can also help. The event could be a concert, gala, farmer's market, in-person tutorials, or other forms of education. Ideally, it will also be supporting other local businesses and entrepreneurs.

You could create a boutique, red carpet type of experience and charge more for tickets, or you could set the price point lower so more people can attend — which helps spread awareness about your project or brand. If your event is super successful, you may even be able to turn it into an annual or monthly event.

From Passion to Profit: 5 Top Tips

Here are some tips to help you be successful when creating a business out of your interests,

1. Find a Mentor or Coach

If you're not really sure how to start turning your passion into profit, consider finding either a business mentor or a coach in your industry who can help you get started. The best way to get money out of your interests is to put money into it! Mentors or coaches can easily be found online with a quick internet search. Make sure you find one that has strong reviews, aligns with your values and is in your budget. You'll also want to meet with the coach or mentor first to make sure that you work well together and get a feel for their personality.

2. Outsource Your Weaknesses

The best thing that you can do for yourself, especially once you can afford to, is to outsource the tasks that you don't enjoy, aren't capable of, or aren't worth your time — which could be better spent elsewhere. Focus on your zone of excellence, and delegate the smaller tasks to a virtual or administrative assistant that can help you out. Often, smaller tasks that a lot of people outsource include social media management, scheduling, email marketing, inbox management, graphic design, and even copywriting.

3. Be Courageous

To successfully start making money from your passion, you need to be courageous and have thick skin throughout the entire process. There will be ups and downs when you're first starting out! There is nothing more important than having the support of others. Join Facebook groups or find other entrepreneurs who can support you in your business goals.

4. Put in the Work

Rome wasn't built in a day, and your new business won't be either. It's going to be grueling work in the beginning, but once the momentum starts going, you'll find success. When you're just starting out, you'll need to market your product, event, services, etc., but the payoff will be worth it in the long run. Stick with it!

5. Schedule Your Day

The key to being successful with any new business is to schedule your workday. A simple way to schedule your day is to use the time blocking method. This essentially means that you guess how long different tasks will take you and then you block that time out on a calendar.

As time goes on, you'll be able to more accurately guess how long each task will take you. Time management and scheduling are important when creating a business.

What is a passion anyway?

"Passion" for most people involves their creativity, their thirst for adventure, an expression of their spirit, a sport, a hobby or an art. Some people want to act, make music, films, write books, travel the world, play sports, perform magic, play videos games, knit or 1000s of other interesting pursuits. Many people want to help others, heal the world, educate and enlighten. These are all wonderful things. But by themselves, they have absolutely no relationship with money. And that is probably one reason why they are so fulfilling and enjoyable. The average human being doesn't dream of spending their days trading stocks or analyzing financial figures.

The average person human being, given no constraints, wants to do things that make him or her feel alive or contribute to others. Most people want money to buy things, but they aren't interested in the mechanisms of the money itself. But we have to look at it closely to understand how to make it.

What is "money," really?
So what is money? "Money" is an agreed upon medium of exchange, given in return for goods and services.Boring, I know. But if you connect the two, a whole world of inspiring (and realistic) possibilities begins to open. The key is to understand that your passion is not just a passion: It is a good or service, ready to be purchased by eager consumers if presented properly. Most passions previously mentioned can fall into two main industries: entertainment and education.

How to connect your passion with the money

Now, instead of just being someone with a passion, you are really an entrepreneur working in one of two industries: entertainment or education. But even with this perspective, making money from your passion was still a distant pipe dream through the 1980s, 1990s, even in the 2000s. Why? Because it was nearly impossible to engage in commerce with either of these industries. If you wanted to provide entertainment to other people in the 1980s, you'd be limited to whatever venues you had nearby. You and your band could perform at the local bar, you could act at the local community theater, and you could potentially pass out flyers and pay a local printing press to make copies of a book (at great expense).

If you wanted to provide education to other people, you could hope there was a college or continuing education company nearby. If you wanted to teach at the college, you'd usually need some kind of expensive academic accreditation and compete for one or two job openings.

These two industries were juggernauts with an iron grip on billions of people's hearts and minds. Multinational corporations controlled all the movie theaters, video-rental stores, bookstores and TV stations in the world. Giant universities controlled all the classrooms and lecture halls in the world. The industries had gatekeepers and millions of passionate artists and educators competing for a few coveted spots. Netflix put Blockbuster video out of business. Amazon drove shopping malls to the brink. Youtube made it possible for average people to become superstars, and Kindle made it possible for the average person to publish their books.

People shifted their attention to their mobile and computer screens, looking at tiny little websites. And unlike NBC or AMC Theaters, you didn't need a multimillion-dollar deal or fame to get onto these websites. You just needed to understand one thing: how to market and package your passion.

Packaging your passion

Sharing your passion in pre-internet days was very difficult:

If you wanted to show people your film, you'd need to carry around nine reels of film and physically load it into a projector. This was of course provided you had the $400,000 to $2 million to make the movie in the first place.

If you wanted to share your music, you'd either need to physically perform for people or pay a huge fee to record a demo and carry copies of the tapes with you or mail them out.

If you wanted to share or sell your book, you had to hire a printing press to physically print up hundreds of copies and hope you sold them all.

Now, with all of the new platforms provided via the internet, it's completely changed:

If your passion is film, you can shoot an independent movie (for less than $400,000) and upload it to Amazon Prime Video and reach millions of people throughout the country and the world. You can work with an aggregator like Filmhub to get on platforms like Google TV and Apple TV, Tubi and Plex.

If your passion is music, you can put your music on Spotify or iTunes with the help of a platform like TuneCore.

If you've written a book, stop hoping to get an agent or publishing deal: Upload it and sell it on Kindle. Not only that, but via print-on-demand technology, Amazon will actually print up individual copies of your book when an individual customer orders it.

If you're a painter, sculptor or other kind of physical artist, you can sell your crafts and creations through your own Etsy store.

If you want to be an educator, you can create an online course about nearly any topic at all, from ballroom dancing to electronic music creation to juggling. You can reach millions of potential students via a site like Udemy.

If you're passionate about any other topic, anything from travel to snowboarding to woodworking, you can start a blog on the topic. You can monetize your blog by selling ads with Google Adsense or promoting other people's products via affiliate marketing.

If you don't want to sell anything, but get paid for creating, you can hire yourself out as a writer, artist, animator, videographer, editor and more via a freelancing marketplace like Upwork.

Marketing your passion

The final piece of the puzzle is something most creators completely overlook, but it's also the most important:

marketing. Many people believe that if they just put their art, creation or course up on a website, people will buy it. That's not true. Have you ever seen Brad Pitt or Margot Robbie on a TV talk show? This isn't done isn't for fun. They are promoting their latest creative project. That's right, even the biggest movie stars on the planet can't just make something and have it sell. They spend weeks and weeks promoting their creations. Movie studios, music labels and book publishers spend millions of dollars every year marketing their products. Fortunately, you don't need a million-dollar budget to market and share your passion products online. Here are a few tips:

Start a dedicated website or blog for your creation. This is a centralized hub you have complete control over and can be a place to not only sell your product or service but also keep in touch with your fans and customers.

Capture your website visitor's emails using an autoresponder service like Mailchimp. There's a saying that "the money is in the list." Consider how powerful it would be if even 50 or 100 people sign up for your list. In real life, it would take hours to personally message all of these people. With an autoresponder, you can message thousands of people with the click of a button.

Give away portions of your creation on social media. Give people a small taste of what you have to share in such a way that it leaves them wanting more. This is what movie trailers do, as well as singles released from popular albums.

Research your audience. Use tools like Ubersuggest to find out the questions and interests they are searching for on Google, and then write content, articles and posts to answer those questions.

Advertise on Google, Facebook and Instagram. For as little as $5 or $10 a day, you can advertise just like major companies and share your creation with a targeted audience. Facebook Ads, for example, let you target people by their likes and interests. So if you are selling music, you can target people who like music similar to yours.

6 STEPS TO TURN YOUR PASSION INTO A CAREER

Are you tired of showing up for work day after day just because you're supposed to? You go not because you want to, but because you have to in order to put food on your table and keep a roof over your head. You've clearly lost that loving feeling for your job and now you don't know what to do about it.If this sounds like you, you're not alone. A study from the Deloitte University Press reported that up to 87.7 percent of America's workforce is not able to contribute to their full potential because they don't have passion for their work. Furthermore, less than 12.3 percent of America's workforce possesses the attributes of worker passion. If you fall into these demographics, maybe it's time to find out what you're really passionate about and turn that into your life's career. Here are six steps to help.

1. Discover your passion.

Your passion should be the thing you enjoy and for which you are naturally wired to excel. There is a huge difference between a hobby and a passion, and it is crucial that you differentiate between the two before quitting your day job. For instance, just because you enjoy painting does not necessarily mean you should make it your profession. You might be better at graphic design, which uses some of the same artistic talents as painting. Keep an open mind and explore all of your options.

2. Determine the demand.

After you have discovered your passion, determine the level of demand for your skills and choose a field. It's risky to plunge into a career with a very low demand, or one with a large number of competitors even though you love it. However, the number of competitors should not be the deal breaker. If you are confident in your skills, it is very possible to establish yourself and compete quite comfortably, as long as you have a strong marketing strategy.

3. Do your research.

Conduct a detailed search on what it would take to launch your career in this field. You may need to acquire specific machinery or equipment, or earn a certification, degree, or special training. You may even need to hire employees or solicit funding. To save headaches later, find out all you can now. Interview people who have or are in a similar business to the one you're considering. Learn what they did to succeed and follow their path, especially if you choose to work in a niche market.

4. Make a plan.

Make a detailed plan of the steps you need to take to make your passion a realistic career opportunity. Include what you need to do and how much you need to spend before you launch into your new venture. If possible, always have a back-up plan in case Plan A doesn't work out.

5. Become qualified.

To be taken seriously, you must first become a professional. Having a special skill may not be enough to deem you an expert, so acquire the training necessary to become marketable. Take a night, weekend or online class while you're in your current job, or a sabbatical to attend an intensive training or internship. As the saying goes, "The more you learn, the more you will earn."

6. Be flexible.

Your road is not always going to be smooth, so plan for hiccups and make adjustments along the way. Be open to advice and criticism; other people's insights may open your eyes to something new. No one can succeed alone. That's why it's important to surround yourself with talented individuals or to form an advisory board to help you make the right decisions. Turning your passion into a career requires motivation. Be proactive and take a step every day that gets you nearer your goal. The fruits of your labor will eventually pay off and you'll be well on your way to doing what you love.

Turn Your Passion Into Profit

Chances are, your full-time job isn't your actual passion. Of course, you'll do something tolerable to pay the bills, but your nine-to-five probably isn't the highlight of your daily life. Some people get lucky, but most wish that they truly loved enough to make a liveable income. The truth is that not every passion can get you rich, but that doesn't mean you shouldn't try. Even a small side business can use your passion and generate some additional income while you get to do something you love doing. So while you won't be quitting your day job any time soon, your life will have a little more color which is worth all the extra effort. Who knows, you might even be able to build a thriving business based on your true passion. Whether it's art, music, woodcarving, or even video games, here are the steps you need to take to turn your passion into profit:

Put it in Your Calendar

The first thing you need to do is make time for your passion. Even if you absolutely love something, a busy schedule full of deadlines and responsibilities will often push your passion to the backburner. To make it a more prominent part of your life, you need to make time for it, even if it means sacrificing part of your weekends or the time you spend watching Netflix after work. When working on your passion projects — write them into your schedule, and it will be easier to commit your valuable time to the work. Otherwise, you'll keep telling yourself that tomorrow will be the day you begin. Add some persistent notifications, and you'll finally start getting to work on that project you keep talking about.

You have a passion for baking but standing in the kitchen is the last thing you want to do when getting home from work. If this is truly your passion, you need to push yourself by scheduling time to bake in your Calendar. You can even schedule times to deliver cookies and cupcakes to friends and family so that you have some sort of deadline or goal to work toward in the early going.

Phone a Friend

Having a partner share your ambitions will drive you further than you could on your own. When you're lacking motivation, they can pick up the slack and help you continue moving forward. The buddy system has worked for countless start-ups and successful projects throughout the years and will work for you today. While a friend can help you turn your passion into a business, you should never rely completely on someone else to make things happen for your work. In the end, you are responsible for making things happen, and if effort starts to falter, you need to look at yourself before pointing fingers. Your friends and family should act as a support system, not your entire engine. To coordinate with a friend who is willing to help, boot up your online Calendar. With Calendar, you can set meetings to create a game plan and set deadlines for each other to complete and share tasks. Using a tool such as Calendar makes sure that you're always on the same page and working toward the same goal.

Find Time to Network

Your friends and family might be supportive of your dreams, but their technical expertise might not be what you need in the later stages of your project development. Let's go back to the baking example. Of course, your loved ones will love when you deliver treats, but how many of them are able to help you create a business model and put it into action? You will likely not know every person who will help you with your business, making it essential to make networking a part of your life. It's extremely important. Through networking, you can find mentors who can guide you in the right direction. For example, if you are a baker, your mentor could be another baker who can talk to you about how they turned a similar passion into their business today. Another networking opportunity might connect you with a wedding planner who can refer many clients to you based on positive interaction.

If you don't know where to start networking, try a social media site such as LinkedIn. You'll be able to read articles from industry experts, engage in conversations, and find like-minded individuals on a similar path as yourself. Later you can find and attend different events and seminars to expand your craft and your business' reach.

Expand Your Business Know-How

To make money from your passion, you need some business know-how. For example, you can be the best musician globally, but without knowing how to market yourself to the world, you won't make much money out of playing. That's why even the greatest artists in the world use agents to grow their brand, but in the beginning, they had to start somewhere. Read articles on starting a business, watch YouTube tutorials, and get to know the stories of entrepreneurs throughout the years. In addition, you'll learn all sorts of valuable tips about salesmanship, product development, social media marketing, and more. These principles, when combined with your skills, will be how your passion can generate a profit. Have you ever thought about online streaming? Thousands of people are trying to earn an income by streaming themselves playing video games to a live audience. Those who succeed are very good at the games they play, but they also have developed a successful brand and marketing strategy that they used to grow their channels. The packaging is just as important, if not more so than the talent.

Continue Practicing

Never stop developing your talents, even when you've made it big. Selling your first record deal doesn't mean you should stop playing the guitar. Instead, it should give you more motivation to keep working and improving. Your

Calendar will always be there to keep you in check even when your passion is starting to see some success as a business model. So keep scheduling time to practice and hone your talents so that your success can endure for years to come. Even if you only make a few extra dollars a month, embracing an entrepreneurial spirit will be beneficial in so many ways in your life. Your passion will become more prominent in your life, and you'll learn so much along the way. So start filling up that Calendar right away and get started!

8 TIPS ON HOW TO TURN YOUR PASSION INTO A BUSINESS YOU CAN MAKE MONEY DOING WHAT YOU LOVE.

Think about the people you know who are great at what they do. More than likely, a passion for their work underpins their performance. That's according to Wes Moore, founder and CEO of the Maryland-based scholastic program, BridgeEdU, a platform he designed out of a passion for reducing dropout rates for college freshman. It's a unique first-year college program that combines core academic courses, internships and service experiences with coaching. Here's his advice on how to turn your passion into a sustainable and scalable business.

1. Find the fault lines surrounding your passion

Look for the holes or things that could be done better within the industry. From there, think about how you can create something sustainable. BridgeEDU came about because Moore had a passion for students who couldn't make it through their freshman year of college. He identified the three main problem areas these people faced-financial aid, academics and a social life-and looked at what solutions already existed and how they could be improved upon. From there, it was just a matter of creating a strong business plan.

2. Become an expert on your industry as well as all aspects of doing business

You need know what you are talking about. Don't say you want to start a circus because you love animals but disregard the fact that you don't understand things such as maintenance, real estate, insurance and marketing. You must know your industry inside and out, as well as how to operate within it.

3. Stop listening to everyone else

Clear your head and don't allow the noise of good intentions shape your life. You can define your own destiny.

4. Don't be a slave to your major

Only 8 percent of people under 35 are working in the field they majored in during college. Don't be afraid to change your path.

5. The moment you grow out of your work role, leave

Every day you do something you are not passionate about, you become increasingly ordinary.

6. Volunteer and sit on boards

Many professional opportunities start here. Networking and the ability to tap different ways of thinking matter.

7. Make sure you have family buy-in

Be with someone who doesn't just love you for who you are, but for who you hope to become.

8. Bring those you are trying to support into the conversation

You must understand their preferences, problems and needs as well as the best ways you can help them. Find ways to open channels of communication with future customers so that you involve them in your thinking and action.

Follow Your Passions, and Success Will Follow

Whether an individual is considering starting a small business or changing career paths, passion must be factored into the equation. While characteristics such as strong values, talent, ambition, intellect, discipline, persistence, and luck all contribute to business and career success, following your passion can often make the most significant difference of all. Before discussing passion and explaining its significance, we must first define the true meaning of success. Success is usually thought of as making large sums of wealth or achieving a certain level of fame, but true success that satisfies is not all about money.

Success is better defined as an achievement of a desired aim or purpose. More than money or fame, most people desire to align their own passions with their work while making a sustainable income. Money brings diminishing returns the more you make, which makes it an elusive definition of success. For most people, success means being proud of their achievements and being part of something that matters. This is particularly true when it comes to meaningful work. If an individual decides to follow their passion, there is a greater likelihood that money and traditional success will follow because the time and effort invested in the venture come with enthusiasm and zeal.

Why Passion Is So Important

If enthusiasm and passion are present, people tend to be more resilient when encountering obstacles. People who are passionate about what they do, rather than just "in it for the money," tend to be people who have more positive outlooks and can overcome difficulty through problem-solving. Also, the more passionate someone is about their job, the more inclined they are to work hard on self-improvement, increasing their chances of success.

Follow Your Passion and Succeed: 4 Icons Who Did

1. Steve Jobs

One of the most successful companies in the world is Apple. Apple's founder and most notable leader was the late Steve Jobs. In an article titled "The Seven Success Principles of

Steve Jobs," writer Carmine Gallo outlines seven factors responsible for Jobs' success. The article is based on interviews with Apple employees and Steve Jobs himself. The first principle? "Do what you love. Steve Jobs believed in the power of passion and once said, "People with passion can change the world for the better."

2. Chris Gardner

Chris Gardner, the once-homeless man, turned multi-millionaire stockbroker featured in the movie The Pursuit of Happyness, expressed what he believes is the secret to success. According to Gardner, the secret is to "find something you love to do so much you can't wait for the sun to rise to do it all over again."

3. Mark Zuckerberg

Mark Zuckerberg, CEO of Meta (formerly Facebook), has changed the world in which we live. In David Kirkpatrick's book The Facebook Effect: The Inside Story of the Company That is Connecting The World, Kirkpatrick lists what he believes are Zuckerberg's characteristics that led to his success. One of these characteristics is following his passion, not money. Zuckerberg suggests "following your happiness" when at a crossroads, using the logic that even if you do not end up making a fortune, you will at least be doing what you love.

4. Warren Buffett

Warren Buffett, known as "the Oracle of Omaha," is probably one of the greatest investors of all time. But even Buffett knows there is more to success than money. In an interview with Parade Magazine, Buffett outlined ten ways to get rich. He concluded his list of advice with, "Know what success really means." He explains the importance of finding what brings true meaning and what makes each day meaningful, which should be the focus of an individual's efforts.

The need for healthcare and a steady income are reasons that many Americans feel compelled to stay where they are. However, if there is a way for a person to navigate the financial hurdles and pursue their passion in a niche area, hard work and success might come easier than assumed. Enjoying the work you do, in some ways, is more important than having a large bank account.

Turning Your Passion Into Profit A Guide to Starting Your Own Business

For some people, their passion is something that they have been interested in since they were young. Others may have a more recent interest that they want to pursue. Regardless of how you found your passion, it is important to remember that your passion is what drives you. It is what makes you excited to get up in the morning and start your day. Your passion is what you love to do. It is what makes you feel alive. When you are pursuing your passion, you are in your element. You are doing what you were meant to do.

Why turn Your Passion Into a business?

There are many reasons why you should turn your passion into a business. First, when you are passionate about something, you are more likely to be successful at it. You will be driven to put in the hard work and dedication required to make your business a success. Second, pursuing your passion can be incredibly rewarding. When you love what you do, it doesn't feel like work. You will be motivated by your desire to succeed, not simply by the paycheck.

Third, starting a business based on your passion can give you a sense of purpose. Your business can be something more than just a way to make money. It can be a way to make a difference in the world.

Fourth, a passion-based business can be a great way to meet new people and build relationships. When you are passionate about something, other people are drawn to you. They want to know more about what you do and why you do it.

Fifth, a business based on your passion can be extremely fulfilling. When you love what you do, it shows in your work. You will be proud of what you have accomplished and feel a deep sense of satisfaction.

How to Turn Your Passion Into a Business

Now that you know why you should turn your passion into a business, its time to learn how to do it. The first step is to define your passion. What are you passionate about? What do you love to do? Once you have answered these questions, you need to find a way to turn your passion into a business. This may require some creativity and outside-the-box thinking. But if you are truly passionate about something, you will find a way to make it happen. Here are a few tips to help you get started:

1. Do Your Research

The first step is to do your research. If you want to turn your passion into a successful business, you need to understand the market and the competition. What is the potential for growth? Who are your target customers? What do they want? How can you reach them?

2. Create a Business Plan

Once you have done your research, its time to create a business plan. This document will outline your goals, strategies, and tactics for making your business a success. It will also help you secure funding and attract investors.

3. Build a Team

No business can succeed without a great team in place. As you start to build your company, surround yourself with people who share your vision and who have the skills and experience necessary to help you achieve your goals.

4. Promote Your Business

Last but not least, don't forget to promote your business. Get the word out there about what you do and why people should care. Use social media, traditional marketing techniques, and any other platform you can think of to reach your target audience.

Defining your passion and turning it into a business - Turning Your Passion Into Profit A Guide to Starting Your Own Business

2. Developing a business plan

When it comes to turning your passion into profit, the first step is always to develop a business plan. This document will outline your business goals, strategies, target market, and financial projections. Without a business plan, it will be difficult to make your business dreams a reality Creating a business plan can seem like a daunting task, but it doesn't have to be. Start by focusing on your business goals. What do you want to achieve with your business? Once you have a good understanding of your goals, you can start to develop strategies for how to achieve them.bYour target market is another important consideration when creating your business plan. Who are your potential customers? What needs do they have that your business can fill? What are your competition's strengths and weaknesses? Answering these questions will help you to develop a marketing plan that will reach your target market.

Finally, you'll need to develop financial projections for your business. This will include estimating your start-up costs, overhead costs, and expected revenue. Financial projections are important to help you understand whether or not your business is feasible. They can also help you to obtain funding from investors or lenders. Developing a business plan may seem like a lot of work, but it's an essential first step in starting your own business. By taking the time to develop a well-thought-out plan, you'll be setting yourself up for success.

3. Conducting market research

When it comes to starting your own business, market research is essential in order to determine whether or not there is a demand for your product or service. This can be done in a number of ways, such as conducting surveys, interviews, and focus groups. Additionally, you can also research your competition to see what they are offering and how they are marketing their business. Once you have gathered this information, you can begin to formulate your business plan. This should include your goals and objectives, as well as your marketing and financial strategies. It is also important to have a realistic idea of the costs associated with starting and running your business.

One of the most important aspects of starting your own business is making sure that you have the passion and drive to see it through. This means that you need to be dedicated to your goals and be willing to put in the hard work required to make your business a success. If you are serious about starting your own business, then it is important to conduct market research and create a solid business plan.

With dedication and hard work, you can turn your passion into profit.

4. Building a strong team

In any business, the people you surround yourself with are critical to your success. As the old saying goes, "You're only as good as the company you keep." When starting your own business, it's important to build a strong team of individuals who share your vision and who will help you turn your passion into profit. There are a few key things to look for when building your team. First, you want to make sure that everyone is on the same page. Everyone should be clear about the goals of the business and what their role is in helping to achieve those goals. It's also important to make sure that your team is diverse. A diverse team brings a variety of skills and perspectives to the table, which can be invaluable in finding creative solutions to problems. Another important thing to look for in team members is a shared commitment to the business. This means that everyone on the team is willing to put in the hard work necessary to make the business a success. This can be difficult to find, but it's worth it to take the time to find people who share your commitment to the business.

Finally, you want to make sure that your team is supportive of one another. This means that they are willing to offer help and advice when needed and that they are also willing to lend a listening ear when needed. A supportive team is essential to a successful business.bBuilding a strong team is essential to any business, but it's especially important when starting your own business. Take the time to find people who share your vision and who are committed to helping you turn your passion into profit.

5. Managing finances

There are a lot of things to think about when you're starting your own business, but one of the most important is how you're going to manage your finances. If you're not careful, it's easy to let your business finances get out of control. That's why it's important to have a plan for how you're going to manage your money. Here are a few tips for managing your finances when you're starting your own business:

1. Keep track of your expenses.

It's important to know where your money is going. Keep track of all of your business expenses so you can see where you're spending the most money.

2. Make a budget.

Once you know where your money is going, you can start to make a budget. Decide how much you want to spend in each area of your business and then stick to it.

3. Get help if you need it.

If you're not sure how to manage your finances, there are plenty of resources available to help you. You can find books, online courses, and even financial advisors who can help you get your business finances under control.

4. Stay organized.

Keeping track of your finances can be a lot easier if you're organized. Use a system that works for you, whether it's a spreadsheet or a budgeting app. And make sure to update it regularly so you always know where your money is going.

5. Be patient.

It takes time to get your business off the ground, and it takes time to get your finances in order. Don't expect everything to be perfect from the start. Just focus on making progress and things will eventually start to fall into place.

Managing finances - Turning Your Passion Into Profit A Guide to Starting Your Own Business

6. Marketing your business

When it comes to marketing your business, it is important to first understand your target market. This can be done by conducting market research. Once you have a good understanding of your target market, you can then begin to develop a marketing strategy. There are many different marketing channels that you can use to reach your target market, such as online marketing, offline marketing, and word-of-mouth marketing. It is important to test out different marketing channels to see what works best for your business. When it comes to online marketing, there are many different options that you can use. Some popular online marketing channels include search engine optimization (SEO), pay-per-click (PPC) advertising, social media marketing, and content marketing. It is important to experiment with different online marketing channels to see which ones work best for your business.

Offline marketing channels include things like print advertising, television advertising, radio advertising, and direct mail. Again, it is important to test out different offline marketing channels to see which ones work best for your business. One of the most important aspects of marketing is to track your results. This can be done by setting up tracking codes on your website or using third-party tracking tools. By tracking your results, you will be able to see which marketing channels are bringing in the most traffic and conversions. This information will help you to optimize your marketing strategy. Hopefully, this guide has given you some helpful tips on how to turn your passion into profit by starting your own business. Remember to conduct market research, develop a marketing strategy, and track your results. With some hard work and dedication, you can be successful in turning your passion into profit.

7. Growing your business

Starting and growing a business takes hard work, dedication, and a bit of luck. But, if you have a great product or service and are passionate about what you do, then you have a much better chance of success. The first step to starting your own business is to come up with a great idea. It should be something that you're passionate about and that you know there is a demand for. Once you have your idea, the next step is to create a business plan. This will help you map out your goals, how you're going to achieve them, and what resources you need.

Once you have your business plan in place, its time to start marketing your business. You need to let people know about what you're offering and why they should choose you over the competition. There are a number of ways to market your business, including online marketing, PR, and advertising. As your business starts to grow, you'll need to start thinking about hiring staff. This will help you take some of the workload off your shoulders and will allow you to focus on other aspects of the business. When hiring staff, its important to find people who share your passion for the business and who will be dedicated to helping it grow. Growing your business takes time, patience, and a lot of hard work. But, if you're passionate about what you do and are willing to put in the effort, then you can achieve success.

8. Overcoming challenges

When you're passionate about something, it can be easy to overlook the challenges involved in turning that passion into a profit-making business venture. But the truth is, any business faces challenges its just a matter of what those challenges are and how you overcome them. One of the first challenges you'll face is coming up with a business idea that's both viable and feasible. You need an idea that solves a problem or meets a need, and one that you can actually execute on. This can be harder than it sounds, but there are plenty of resources out there to help you brainstorm and validate your business idea, including lean canvases and business model templates.

Once you have your idea, the next challenge is putting together a team. If you're going it alone, you'll need to wear all the hats yourself, which can be tough. But even if you have a co-founder or partners, you'll still need to identify the key roles that need to be filled and find people with the right skillsets to fill them. This includes everything from designers and developers to marketers and salespeople. Another big challenge is funding. Unless you have deep pockets or investors lined up, you'll need to get creative with how you finance your business. This might mean bootstrapping it from the start or looking for alternative sources of funding like crowdfunding or grants. And then there's the challenge of actually building and launching your product or service. This can be tricky even for experienced entrepreneurs, so its important to have a clear plan and timeline in place. It also helps to build in some flexibility, as things will inevitably come up that you didn't anticipate.

Last but not least, you need to promote and market your business effectively if you want to succeed. This means figuring out who your target market is and what channels you should use to reach them. It also requires creating compelling content and marketing materials, as well as staying active on social media and other online platforms. All of these challenges can seem daunting, but the good news is that they can be overcome with planning, preparation, and perseverance. So if you're ready to turn your passion into profit, don't let anything stand in your way start planning your business today.

9. Making your passion profitable

When it comes to turning your passion into profit, there are a few key things to keep in mind. First and foremost, you need to be clear about your goals and what you hope to achieve by starting your own business. Are you looking to make a full-time income? Or are you simply hoping to supplement your current income and add some extra spending money to your household budget? Once you know your goals, you can start to put together a business plan that will help you achieve them. One of the most important aspects of any business plan is your target market. Who are you going to sell your products or services to? And how are you going to reach them? You need to have a clear understanding of your target market before you can start to market your business to them.

Another important thing to keep in mind when starting your own business is the competition. Who else is doing what you're doing? What are they doing well? What could you do better? Researching your competition is a crucial step in ensuring that your business is successful. Last but not least, you need to have a realistic understanding of the costs associated with starting and running your own business. There are a lot of expenses that go into starting a business, from the cost of goods or services to marketing and advertising expenses. Make sure you have a handle on all of the potential costs before you get started so that you don't end up in over your head. With these things in mind, you're well on your way to turning your passion into profit. Just remember to take things slow and steady, do your research, and always keep your goals in mind. With a little hard work and dedication, you can make your dream of owning your own business a reality.

CONCLUSION

There really is no better way to earn an income than by doing something you love. No matter what you're interested in, there's a way you can turn that passion into profits. If you work hard, surround yourself with the right people, and have the right mindset, there's no reason you won't succeed!

www.ingramcontent.com/pod-product-compliance
Lightning Source LLC
Chambersburg PA
CBHW060843260726
48661CB00002B/586